To our loving
Granddaughter
Peach Blossom
From her
Grandparents Vaughns
& Christmas, 2001

This book belongs to:

_____

Growing with Jesus

100 Daily Devotionals

WRITTEN & ILLUSTRATED BY

Andy Holmes

Watercolor by Sheila Ninowski

Tommy
NELSON

Thomas Nelson, Inc.
Nashville

Published in Nashville, Tennessee, by Tommy Nelson™,
a division of Thomas Nelson, Inc.

Library of Congress Cataloging-in-Publication Data
Holmes, Andy.
    Growing with Jesus: 100 daily devotionals/by Andy Holmes.
      p. cm.
    Summary: A collection of devotional readings comprised of Bible verses, thoughts to
grow on, and amazing facts about the world, designed to promote spiritual growth.
    ISBN 0-8499-5908-X
    1. Youth—Prayer-books and devotions—English. 2. Christian life—juvenile literature.
[1. Prayer books and devotions.] I. Title.
BV4850.H64 2000
242'.62—dc21   99-013589

Printed in the United States of America

01 02 03 04 WCT 9 8 7 6

To Sandy Noe
You're an inspiration to us all to grow with Jesus.

Contents

△ ● ■ △ ○ ■ △ ○ ■

Acknowledgments

A special thanks goes first to Laura Minchew. Without her, this book might never have seen the light of day. My thanks to all the staff at Tommy Nelson. Including (but not limited to) Beverly Phillips and Karen Phillips (no, they're not related). Having a "Tommy Nelson™ book" is the fulfillment of a longtime personal goal. Many thanks go to June Ford for countless phone calls to keep everything moving along — and for lots of great trivia ideas (I love the humpback whale one). Also, my thanks to my sister, Libby, for hand-transferring each illustration onto watercolor paper. Which brings me to Sheila: "Great job!" I absolutely want to thank my wonderful wife, Wendy, for constant encouragement and praise. She honestly thinks I'm great. Cool. I love you more than I did the day I first saw you — and I didn't think that was possible. Thanks to my big boys, Shelton and Andrew. You're the best! And an early "pre-hello" to the little one God is busily knitting together inside Wendy's tummy. Can't wait to meet you! Big-time thanks to Mrs. Peggy Langford, the incredibly kind, helpful, and enthusiastic librarian for the Alta Vista Elementary School in Abilene, Texas. You were so helpful to me. I can't thank you enough for all the books you lent me. Last, to my brother-in-law, John Taylor, who spent hours on-line researching elusive pieces of fascinating trivia from one side of the world to the other. You gave me a much-needed second wind. I truly appreciate it.

Introduction

By the time you finish this book you may have :

- grown an inch taller
- survived two or more haircuts
- outgrown your shoes
- increased your pants size
- clipped your fingernails six times
- completely replaced the outer layer of your skin (four times!), and
- worn out 120,000,000 of your body's cells (and automatically replaced them with brand-new ones)!

You will also have grown in *invisible* ways. That's right—on the *inside*. How do I know? Because God designed you that way.

The act of growing is very important to God. You can see it in almost everything he made. Animals grow. Fish grow. Plants grow.

Like you, most things begin very, very small. Look at you now!

You can run.
You can jump.
You can climb.
You can read.
You can draw.
You can imagine.

And by the time you finish this book, you should be able to do these things even better! Why do I say *should*? Because that is partly up to you.

No, you can't make your hair stop growing or force your body to stay the same size, but you can slow things down on the *inside*. How? By making wrong choices.

Will you choose to grow on the *inside*? If so, you'll love this book. It will help you grow up God's way from the *inside* out. Along the way you will also learn a brainload of fun, weird, and fascinating things about your amazing body and about the amazing world we live in.

Are you ready? Then turn the next page!

You're God's Special Project

△ ● ■ △ ○ ■ △ ○ ■

BIBLE VERSES

"You [God] made my whole being. You formed me in my mother's body. I praise you because you made me in an amazing and wonderful way."

PSALM 139:13–14

Thoughts to Grow On:

Have you ever made something you really liked? A drawing, an invention, or a special project? You probably kept it in a place where everyone could see it and where it would be safe. Can you remember how pleased you felt?

Guess what? God feels the same way about you—only a zillion times stronger! He knows that no two of his children are alike. God is happy with you. God not only loves you; he *likes* you. God is proud of you and wants to present you to the whole world.

Today:

Look in your mirror and say, "Hello, child of the King!" Say it five times, and believe it because you *are* a child of the King.

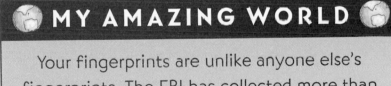

MY AMAZING WORLD

Your fingerprints are unlike anyone else's fingerprints. The FBI has collected more than 170 million fingerprints and has *never* found two that are alike.

On Butterfly Wings

△⬤◻️◺◯◼️◺◯◻️

BIBLE VERSE

If anyone belongs to Christ, then he is made new.
The old things have gone; everything is made new!

2 CORINTHIANS 5:17

Thoughts to Grow On:

Have you ever seen a caterpillar spin itself into a cocoon? An amazing thing is quietly happening inside that silky womb: The caterpillar is being *transformed* into a butterfly.

God is working an even more amazing transformation in you! And you don't have to curl up inside a cocoon to experience it. God is transforming the "regular you" into the "new creation you." That "new creation you" can do something the "regular you" could never do—it can be like Jesus!

Today:
Draw or find a picture of a butterfly. Let it remind you of the wonderful changes God is working in you.

🌎 MY AMAZING WORLD 🌎

There are several thousand species (different kinds) of the butterfly. Some species of butterfly grow in the "pupa" (or "cocoon") for several months while other species make their transformation into a butterfly within a few days.

A Farmer's Life

△◉▣◮◬○◼◮○▣

BIBLE VERSE

Do not be fooled: You cannot cheat God. A person harvests only what he plants.

GALATIANS 6:7

Thoughts to Grow On:

Have you *ever* heard of a farmer planting corn seed to grow tomatoes? Of course not. Things simply do not work that way. If you want to harvest tomatoes, you'd better plant *tomato* seeds.

The same is true with your life. If you want your life to be truly good, plant the seeds of godly words, godly thoughts, and godly actions in your heart and mind.

Today:

Imagine yourself as a farmer.
Think of your mind as your field.
What kind of seeds are you
going to plant?

🌍 MY AMAZING WORLD 🌍

A giant sequoia tree in California is the biggest
living thing in the world. It is almost 3,000
years old, 275 feet high, and its trunk is 79 feet
wide! Picture it this way: That's as tall as a
second Statue of Liberty standing on the
shoulders of the real Statue of Liberty,
and is almost as wide as three city buses
parked bumper to bumper!

Thank You! Thank You! Thank You!

△ ◗ ▢ △ ◯ ◼ △ ◯ ▢

BIBLE VERSE

Give thanks whatever happens.

1 THESSALONIANS 5:18

Thoughts to Grow On:

I'm sure you can easily cheer, "Thank you, God!" when fun and exciting things come your way. But what do you do during the hard times? How do you act during the bad times?

Do you groan?

Do you complain?

Do you whine or throw a fit?

8

Jesus has a better way.
Be thankful. If you'll let him,
Jesus will help you find
something to be thankful for
in every situation—even in your
worst times.

Today:
No matter what happens say, "Thank you, God!"

 MY AMAZING WORLD

International studies have shown that people
all over the world make the same facial
expressions to express basic emotions such as
anger, fear, sadness, and joy. So remember:
Your face often "tells it all."

Jonah's Fish and Tips

△◖▢△◯◼△◖▢

BIBLE VERSE

"So love your enemies. Do good to them, . . ."

LUKE 6:35

Thoughts to Grow On:

Do you remember the story of Jonah? He's the guy who was swallowed by the fish. Do you know that Jonah's biggest problem wasn't the gigantic fish? It was his heart. Jonah didn't want to share God's love with people he didn't like, because he knew that if he did God would forgive them and they wouldn't be destroyed.

God taught Jonah how to love his enemies.

Have you ever wanted bad things to happen to someone you didn't like? Take a tip from what God taught Jonah: Always remember that God loves everyone.

Today:
Do something kind for someone you don't like.

🌎 MY AMAZING WORLD 🌎

Sharks' teeth grow in rows in their gums. Behind the front row of teeth is a second row of teeth. When the front teeth wear out, they are immediately replaced by a brand-new second row of teeth. A tiger shark can go through as many as 24,000 teeth in ten years.

Complaint Department Closed

△ ● ■ ◢ ○ ■ ◢ ○ ■

BIBLE VERSE

Do everything without complaining or arguing.

PHILIPPIANS 2:14

Thoughts to Grow On:

Let's do an experiment.

Step 1

- Scrunch your eyebrows downward.
- Turn your lips downward.
- Tighten your arms across your chest.
- Sigh heavily.
- Grumble, "It's too hard!" five times.

Step 2

- Relax your face.
- Raise your eyebrows.
- Smile.
- Shout, "I can do it!" five times.

Did you feel the difference? It takes far more energy to be negative than it does to be positive. That's why being a grump is so exhausting!

Today:

Greet every chore, challenge, duty, and task with a positive attitude.

🌎 MY AMAZING WORLD 🌎

It has been estimated that it takes 72 muscles to frown and only 15 muscles to smile.

Above and Beyond

△●□△○■△●□

BIBLE VERSE

"Those [people] who give mercy to others are happy.
Mercy will be given to them."

Matthew 5:7

Thoughts to Grow On:

Imagine you've made a horrible mistake. However, when you tell your folks about it they say, "That's okay. We'll give you another chance."

Imagine how relieved you would feel. It would seem as if the weight of the whole world had been taken off your shoulders. You deserved to be punished but were given *mercy* instead.

14

Today:

Listen. Jesus is talking to you today. He's telling you to show the same mercy to those who have wronged you. Does anyone come to mind? How could you show that person mercy?

MY AMAZING WORLD

On August 16, 1996, at Chicago's Brookfield Zoo, a female gorilla named "Binti" shocked the world when she rescued and gently cuddled a 3-year-old boy who had accidentally fallen into the gorilla exhibit. Binti, who was carrying her own baby gorilla on her back during the merciful rescue, brought the boy to the zookeeper's entrance of her cage where helpers were able to take the child to safety.

Eat It Up

△⬤▢△◯▣△◯▢

BIBLE VERSE

"Blessed are those who hunger and thirst for righteousness, for they shall be filled."

MATTHEW 5:6 (NKJV)

Thoughts to Grow On:

Have you ever heard your tummy groan or grumble? That's your body's way of saying, "Hello up there! I need some food!"

Have you ever been so thirsty that your mouth felt as dry as the desert sand? Remember how wonderful it was when you finally found a glass of water and guzzled it down?

God wants you to be *hungry* for him. God wants you to *thirst* for him. Think of God as *food* for your spirit and living *water* for your soul.

Today:
Say this prayer aloud:

> *Dear God,*
> *Teach me to be hungry for you.*
> *Teach me to be thirsty for your Word.*
> *Thank you, Lord.*
> *Amen.*

 MY AMAZING WORLD

The human body can go 40-plus days without food, possibly four days without water, but less than four minutes without oxygen (air).

Against the Flow

△ ● ▢ △ ○ ■ △ ○ ▢

BIBLE VERSE

"Those [people] who are treated badly for doing good are happy. The kingdom of heaven belongs to them."

MATTHEW 5:10

Thoughts to Grow On:

Jesus lived his life doing only good things, yet think of how horribly he was treated. He was spit on, laughed at, and beaten. Finally, he was arrested and put to death as a criminal.

What will *you* do when kids make fun of you for doing the right thing? Decide today to stand strong—even if your best friend turns against you.

God will give you the power to make it through these tough times and reward you with his joy.

Today:

Spy on yourself! Pay close attention to the things you say and do. Make sure you are a *leader* for good things instead of being a follower of bad things.

🌎 MY AMAZING WORLD 🌎

In the wild, horses live in herds (groups) with one horse serving as "chief stallion." The chief stallion is the most fit leader, able to guide and protect the herd.

Good-bye, Guilt.
Hello, Happiness!

△⬤▢△◯▣△⬤▢

BIBLE VERSE

"When our hearts make us feel guilty, we can still have
peace before God. God is greater than our hearts,
and he knows everything."

1 JOHN 3:20

Thoughts to Grow On:
Guilt is that nagging, yucky
feeling you get after you've
done something *wrong*.
Think of guilt as the rotting
scraps in your kitchen
garbage pail. If you let
them stay in there,
they will turn sour
and stink. The secret
sins you hide in your

heart rot and turn sour, too. They will rob you of happiness.

Guess what? The *only way* to no longer feel guilty is to no longer hide the wrong thing you've done. God says, "I love you. Don't be afraid to tell me about it." And what's more, God knows all about it already. And the best news is that he's not waiting to *scold* you, he's waiting to *hold* you and give you his peace.

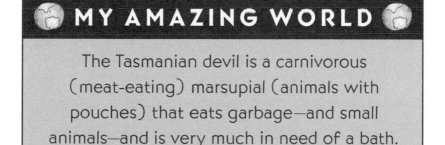

Today:
Tell God about the wrong things you've done. Do it right now.

🌎 MY AMAZING WORLD 🌎

The Tasmanian devil is a carnivorous (meat-eating) marsupial (animals with pouches) that eats garbage—and small animals—and is very much in need of a bath. It is possible to smell one miles away.

Remember the Lord

△◉▢△○▣△○▢

BIBLE VERSE

Remember the Lord in everything you do. And he
will give you success.

PROVERBS 3:6

Thoughts to Grow On:

Imagine you're getting ready
to go to school. Think
through a checklist of what
you'd need to do.

✓ Get out of bed.

✓ Get dressed.

✓ Eat breakfast.

✓ Brush your teeth and hair.

✓ Grab your school backpack
(and lunch).

Now you're ready. Right?
Wait. There's one more thing:

✓ Tell God "Good morning"
and thank him for being with
you throughout the day.

If you remember God in all that you do, he has
promised to give you success. That doesn't mean
he'll give you A's on your tests when you haven't
studied. It means that God will give you strength,
wisdom, and courage to successfully handle every
minute of your day.

Today:
Remember the Lord in all your activities.

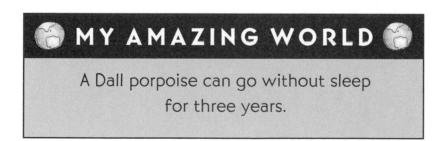

🌍 **MY AMAZING WORLD** 🌍

A Dall porpoise can go without sleep
for three years.

Do Your Best

△ 🥚 ● ◼ △ ○ ◼ △ ● ◼

BIBLE VERSE

"Whatever work you do, do your best."

ECCLESIASTES 9:10

Thoughts to Grow On:
Get out a pencil and a piece of paper.

Part 1. Hold your pencil firmly. Pay close attention to what you're doing. In your very best handwriting, write: I am doing my best.

Part 2. Hold your pencil very loosely. Gaze into mid-air and slouch. Once again, write: I am doing my best.

Study the two sentences. Which line turned out best? The first one, of course! Why? Because you *truly* did your best. In the second one, you did *just enough to get by*.

God wants you to do your best in everything you try.

Today:

Determine to do your best in everything you do. But beware! You'll enjoy the rewards so much you'll never want to do anything halfway again.

🌎 MY AMAZING WORLD 🌎

A honeybee makes 154 trips to make just one teaspoonful of honey. In order to gather a pound of honey, a bee flies a distance equal to more than three trips around the world.

God Never Gives Up on You

△◉■△○■△◉■

BIBLE VERSE

God began doing a good work in you. And he will continue it until it is finished when Jesus Christ comes again.

PHILIPPIANS 1:6

Thoughts to Grow On:

Have you ever started something and then given up? Maybe you grew bored with it. Maybe you thought you'd never finish it and you became discouraged. Maybe you really *wanted* to finish it, but you didn't know how.

God has started a good work in you. He has *determined* to make you pleasing to him in *every* way. He wants to train you to love the way he loves, to forgive the way he forgives, and to do good just as he does good.

So don't worry if you make mistakes along the way (even the same mistakes). God will not give up on you. Ever.

Today:
Thank God for his promise to always help you in *every* way.

🌍 MY AMAZING WORLD 🌍

A beautiful pearl begins as a grain of sand. The grain of sand enters the shell of an oyster, mussel, or clam and gets covered (and strengthened) with layer after layer of *nacre* The process takes at least three years.

God Rewards for Good Behavior

△ ⬤ ▢ △ ◯ ■ △ ◯ ▢

Remember that the Lord will give a reward to everyone, slave or free, for doing good.

EPHESIANS 6:8

Thoughts to Grow On:

Have you ever done a job and been paid for it? Some kids rake leaves, some clean garages, some take care of a vacationing neighbor's pet. But can you imagine being paid for simply being kind? Guess what? The Bible says you will be rewarded.

God has promised to *reward* everyone for the

good things they do. And he'll reward you with something you can never lose through a hole in your pocket. God will reward you with his *joy*. He will pour his laughter into your heart, and you will grin from ear to ear. Try it out and see for yourself.

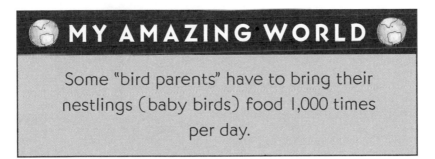

Today:
Be a "do-gooder."

🌍 MY AMAZING WORLD 🌍

Some "bird parents" have to bring their nestlings (baby birds) food 1,000 times per day.

All Kinds of Prayers

△ ● ■ △ ○ ■ △ ● □

BIBLE VERSE

Pray with all kinds of prayers, and ask for everything you need.

EPHESIANS 6:18

Thoughts to Grow On:

Do you cheer when you're bored? Do you whine when you're happy? Do you whistle when you're angry? Or dance when you're feeling blue? No way, right? Why? Because you have lots of different ways to express your many feelings.

Are you ready for a news flash? God wants you to share *all* of your feelings with him.

Pray when you're feeling silly.
Pray when you're feeling bored.
Pray when you're not really
feeling anything in particular. Glad, sad, mad, or, yes,
even bad, God loves *your* company.

Today:

See how many times you can talk to God today.
And remember, whether you whisper or roar, God is
always ready to listen.

MY AMAZING WORLD

Your voice is like a musical instrument. Instead
of using your fingers to change the sounds an
instrument makes, your vocal cords may take as
many as 170 different positions!

I'm So Mad!

BIBLE VERSE

Do not become angry easily.

JAMES 1:19

Thoughts to Grow On:

How often do you get angry? Once a week? Once a day? Once an hour?

It's okay to get mad—even *really* mad. Remember when Jesus chased the money-changers out of the temple? He was *very* angry. But when you look closely at Jesus' life you find that he didn't become angry *easily*.

Do you want to grow with Jesus today? Then *determine* to be *slow to anger*. If something gets under your skin, step back; take a deep breath; count to ten; or leave the room until you calm down enough to *think clearly*; and *talk with kindness* about whatever it is that has upset you.

Today:

If something gets you mad, use self-control.

 MY AMAZING WORLD

Sloths have a top speed of one mile per hour, making them the slowest of all mammals. Why are they so slow? Their arms and legs are too weak to support their bodies.

Make Peace with Others

△◗▢◿◯◼◿◯▢

BIBLE VERSE

Finally, all of you should live together in peace.

1 PETER 3:8

Thoughts to Grow On:

Think of someone you really like to spend time with. No doubt, you both like many of the same things. After all, that's partly why you're such good friends. But do you *always* want to do the same things? Probably not. Is this okay? Absolutely!

So how will you handle those times when you want to do different things? With a smile

and an extra dose of generosity. And if it's one of those things you feel like parting ways over, remind yourself how much you love each other, then kindly *agree to disagree*. If you want to keep the friendship, you have to keep the peace.

Today:

Determine to be a peacemaker.

MY AMAZING WORLD

The moon doesn't *shine*. It has no light of its own. It acts more like a mirror and reflects the sun's light.

Do Not Be Jealous

△ ◉ ▢ △ ○ ▣ △ ○ ▢

BIBLE VERSE

Do not be jealous or speak evil of others.

1 PETER 2:1

Thoughts to Grow On:

How do you feel when you see someone getting something you'd like to have? Does it bother you inside, or are you truly happy for them?

It's easy to become jealous when others get something you want, but jealousy only hurts you. Jealous feelings work like a horrible disease that infects your whole body. Soon, you're full of bitterness from your head to your toes.

36

Next time you begin to feel jealous, stop yourself. Concentrate on how happy you'd be if *it* had been *you* instead of *them*. Then switch that excitement back over to them.

Today:
Decide to be happy when good things happen to someone *else*.

In 1439, in an effort to slow down the spread of disease, King Henry VI banned *kissing*.

Think about Jesus

△ ◐ ▣ △ ○ ◼ △ ◐ ▢

BIBLE VERSE

So all of you, holy brothers, should think about Jesus.

HEBREWS 3:1

Thoughts to Grow On:

Sometimes it's hard to think about Jesus when you're away from church. After all, you've never *really* met him in *real life*. You don't know what he sounded like. You don't even know what he really looked like.

Yet, those are not important things. The important thing is to know Jesus' heart. When you think about Jesus, think about:

1. **How *kind* he was.** He always looked for the best in people. So can you.

2. **How *powerful* he was.** He made sick people well and raised Lazarus from the dead! He will help you, too.

3. **How much he *loves* you.** He died a horrible death on the cross, so that God and you could be best friends. You can accept his friendship today!

Today:

Make this a *happy* thinking day!

MY AMAZING WORLD

Your brain weighs less than three pounds, is about the size of a grapefruit, and is thousands of times more powerful than the world's most powerful computer.

Be Satisfied

BIBLE VERSE

And be satisfied with what you have.

HEBREWS 13:5

Thoughts to Grow On:

Do you remember the story *The Emperor's New Suit*? He was never satisfied and always had to have more clothes. His love for always having the "latest and greatest" fashions soon led him to make a royal fool of himself.

Don't be fooled into loving *things*. *Use* things. Love *people*. What's in style today will be out of style tomorrow. And that toy or shirt you've been dreaming about will soon break, wear out, or lose its appeal.

Love people instead. Think of ways to show others you care. Be thankful and *satisfied* with the things you have.

Today:

Take one item off your secret I-can't-live-without-it list and never crave it again.

Be a Doer

△ ● ▢ △ ○ ▣ △ ○ ▢

BIBLE VERSE

But Jesus said, "Those who hear the teaching of God and obey it—they are the ones who are truly blessed."

LUKE 11:28

Thoughts to Grow On:

Imagine you've been given a wonderful gift that came wrapped in an unusual package. In order to get to the gift—without ruining it—you would have to follow special directions. Would you ignore the directions and eagerly rip into the package, or would you carefully follow the directions?

God has given you just such a gift. It's called *life*. Your life has to be "unwrapped" one choice at a time.

If you make a bad choice, you damage this precious gift. Good choices bring blessings. If you make one bad choice after another, you may destroy this gift altogether.

Today:

Make *God-pleasing* choices today, so that you may *fully* enjoy his gift of life.

🌎 MY AMAZING WORLD 🌎

Three babies are born every second around the world. That's 180 babies in the next minute—10,800 in the next hour!

Jesus' Lunch Menu

△ ⬤ ⬛ △ ◯ ◼ △ ◯ ⬜

BIBLE VERSE

Jesus said, "My food is to do what the One who sent me wants me to do."

JOHN 4:34

Thoughts to Grow On:

Have you ever gone without eating for so long that your stomach growled? Do you remember how good you felt once you ate?

Once Jesus sat beside a well waiting for his disciples to return with lunch. A woman came to draw water. Jesus began talking to her. He told her about God's love. It totally changed her life.

When the disciples returned, they were surprised to hear Jesus tell them he was no longer hungry.

"I have food you don't know about," he said. His food was *doing God's work.*

Today:

Let your hunger pains remind you of God today. Thank him for giving you the *living bread:* Jesus Christ.

 MY AMAZING WORLD

Every minute 500,000 cells of your stomach's lining die and must be replaced. The entire lining is renewed every three days.

Stay Away from Evil

△ ● ■ △ ○ ■ △ ● ■

> ### BIBLE VERSE
>
> Stay away from the evil things young people
> love to do.
>
> 2 TIMOTHY 2:22

Thoughts to Grow On:

Have you ever felt pressured by a
friend to do something you knew
(or *felt*) was wrong?

It takes a lot of courage to hold
out your hands and say "no"
when people you really like are
begging you to follow along and do
something wrong. And though it
may not seem like a big deal to join
in, it *is* a big deal. Why? Because you
are going *against your conscience.*
That's like slamming a wrecking

ball into your heart. The destruction is real, and the wall can only be rebuilt one brick at a time.

Don't let someone else determine your behavior. Make your own choices. You'll be surprised at how powerful you feel when you *think for yourself*.

Today:

Will you wear your thinking cap today and make your own choices?

MY AMAZING WORLD

Your heart pumps about 72 times a minute, or 40 million times a year!

Don't Say Dirty Words

△●■△○■△○■

BIBLE VERSE

Also, there must be no evil talk among you.
You must not speak foolishly or tell evil jokes.
These things are not right for you.

EPHESIANS 5:4

Thoughts to Grow On:

Do you remember the
first time you heard
someone tell a dirty joke
or say a dirty word? Deep
down, you felt sneaky
because you knew you
were hearing something
that shouldn't be said.
Dirty jokes and dirty words
may seem harmless but
they're not.

Imagine throwing a handful of mud into a pitcher of water. The mud would ruin the water immediately by *contaminating* it. The water wouldn't be pure anymore.

Telling dirty jokes or saying dirty words is like throwing mud into your mind—it *contaminates* it. Instead, God says to use your mouth to say *good* things that will help those who hear.

Today:
Practice using your mouth to say only good things.

🌍 MY AMAZING WORLD 🌍

A grown-up's tongue has 9,000 taste buds. A youth's tongue has more taste buds than an adult's. As people grow older they lose some of their ability to taste.

Have Patience

△⬤⬛△◯⬛△◯⬛

BIBLE VERSE

And we also have joy with our troubles because we
know that these troubles produce patience.

ROMANS 5:3

Thoughts to Grow On:

Patience might sound like
something a grown-up needs
(and they do!), but you
need it, too. Why? Because
you have to wait for stuff,
too. And that *waiting*—
when done with calmness
and self-control instead of
with whining and
complaining—is called
patience.

SNAIL
RACES

Patience makes your life easier and more enjoyable. It keeps you from driving yourself (or others!) crazy while you wait for things you're eager for, such as your birthday or Christmas.

Today:

Start practicing patience. If you find you have to wait around for something, make a *choice* to do it with calmness and a good, easy-to-get-along-with attitude.

🌎 MY AMAZING WORLD 🌎

The peanut buries its own seeds, which—after a long, slow growing season—produces new peanuts and so guarantees its survival.

Wisdom from God

BIBLE VERSE

But if any of you needs wisdom, you should
ask God for it.

JAMES 1:5

Thoughts to Grow On:

Wisdom is a word you probably
don't use very often. Some
people think it means *to be
smart*, but the Bible says,
"Wisdom begins with respect
for the Lord" (Psalm 111:10).

Without wisdom you will do many
foolish things.

"Wisdom will help you be a good
person. It will help you do what is
right" (Proverbs 2:20).

How do you get wisdom? You ask God for it because that's where it comes from. *And you keep on asking God for it*. You *seek after it* as if you were searching for silver. You hunt for it as if you were looking for hidden treasure. Why? Because that's exactly what wisdom is—a treasure.

Today:

Begin asking God for *wisdom*.

MY AMAZING WORLD

King Solomon's gift of wisdom from God was so great people from all over the world—including the Queen of Sheba—came to hear him speak.

Don't Argue

△ ● ▪ △ ○ ▪ △ ● ▪

BIBLE VERSE

Stay away from foolish and stupid arguments.

2 TIMOTHY 2:23

Thoughts to Grow On:

"Is not!"

"Is too!"

You've probably said these words yourself. If so, you know that little arguments become big arguments, and soon you're so angry you never want to talk with each other again.

Before arguing, stop and ask yourself: Is this worth

fighting over? About 99.9 percent of the time, it isn't worth a fight. Then soften your voice and say, "Let's

work this out peacefully. Okay?" Next, you *listen*. Try to *see the other person's side*. If that doesn't solve the problem, find someone who can listen to both sides fairly. And ask for God's help. He'll show you how to please him.

Today:
Try not to argue at all.

🌍 MY AMAZING WORLD 🌍

Talk about getting along! A single colony of ants may have as many as 20 million individuals.

You Have a Special Gift

△ ⬮ ◻ △ ○ ◼ △ ○ ◻

Christ gave each one of us a special gift. Each one received what Christ wanted to give him.

EPHESIANS 4:7

Thoughts to Grow On:

Have you ever been at a friend's birthday party and secretly wished you had been given one of the gifts your friend got? Or, have you wished you had a talent or an ability someone else has but you don't?

Guess what? Jesus gave you the gift he wanted you to

have. The gifts didn't get mixed up or delivered to the wrong people. Christ has given a special gift to you so that you will use it for him.

Today:
Read 1 Corinthians 12:4–31. It will help you learn about your special gift.

 MY AMAZING WORLD

At least ten million other people have the same birthday as you. If your birthday is in April, May, or June, you share your birthday with even more people.

Firstfruits Belong to God

△◐▢△○▣△●▢

BIBLE VERSE

Honor the Lord by giving him part of your wealth.
Give him the firstfruits from all your crops.

PROVERBS 3:9

Thoughts to Grow On:

This verse is talking about your money. If your allowance is one dollar, give God the *first* ten cents, twenty cents, or even fifty cents. If you find a five-dollar bill on your way home, give God some money *first*. If your grandmother gives you twenty dollars on your birthday, *first* set some aside for God, then enjoy the rest.

You can put God's part of your
money in the offering at
church, send it to a missionary,
or give it to help poor people.
The amount you give is up to you.
Ask God to give you a generous heart
and to help you not to become stingy. Give it
happily, because God loves a *cheerful* giver.

Today:

Practice generosity today.

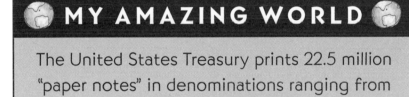

🌍 MY AMAZING WORLD 🌍

The United States Treasury prints 22.5 million
"paper notes" in denominations ranging from
$1 bills to $100 bills.

Don't Brag

△ ◉ ▢ △ ○ ◼ △ ◉ ▢

Don't praise yourself. Let someone else do it.
PROVERBS 27:2

Thoughts to Grow On:

Have you ever been around a braggart? They may boast, "I'm the fastest runner"; "I have the biggest house on the block"; "The teacher likes me the best"; or, "I'm the tallest person in the school!"

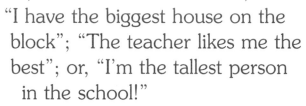

Thank You, God!

SPELLING BEE CHAMPION

It may seem like braggarts are the happiest people on earth, but they're not. Inside, they don't feel special at all. People who brag are secretly saying, "*Please*, think I'm important. *Please*, think I'm special."

God has made each person in a wonderful way. This includes YOU. Your abilities and talents are *gifts* from God. Enjoy them, develop them, and thank God for them. Let other people brag about them. And when they do, remember who gave them to you: God.

Today:

Brag on someone else.

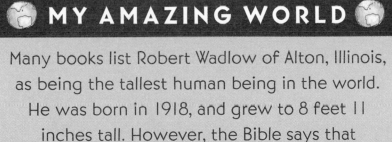

🌐 MY AMAZING WORLD 🌐

Many books list Robert Wadlow of Alton, Illinois, as being the tallest human being in the world. He was born in 1918, and grew to 8 feet 11 inches tall. However, the Bible says that Goliath was even taller, measuring in at a whopping 9 feet 9 inches!

God Works in Everything for Good

△⬤▢△◯■△◯▢

BIBLE VERSE

We know that in everything God works for the good of those who love him.

ROMANS 8:28

Thoughts to Grow On:

Life can get hard sometimes. There are periods in every person's life when they feel like their whole world is falling apart. These are frustrating times, and they can make you want to quit trying altogether.

Maybe someone is blaming you for something you didn't do, or maybe you keep getting overlooked in something you're good at. Whatever it is, one thing is sure: God is working in it *for your good.*

Your heavenly Father knows how many hairs are on your head, and he definitely knows what you're going through. Cling to him and trust that he will bring you through it.

Today:
Give your concerns to God.

 MY AMAZING WORLD

Chicken Little was right. He's the make-believe chicken who, fearing the world was falling apart, went around clucking, "The sky is falling! The sky is falling!" Although there is no reason to worry about it, millions of teeny specks of dust from stars fall to the earth every day and close to 1,500 larger "space-rocks" fall to the ground each year.

God Listens to Me

BIBLE VERSE

I love the Lord because he listens to
my prayers for help.

PSALM 116:1

Thoughts to Grow On:
Think of how special you would
feel if an important official or
even a king asked you to come
and visit with him. It would be a
very rare privilege, something
that most people would never
have an opportunity to do.

An amazing thing has
happened! The Creator of the
whole world has invited YOU
to talk to him—any time, day
or night. And what's even

more amazing, he has promised to *listen*.

Do you have exciting news? God wants to hear about it. Did your best friend move away? Share your feelings with God. No matter what it is, God is right there with his ears (and arms) wide open.

Today:
Spend one whole minute talking to God.

Josiah, the "boy king," became king of Judah when he was only eight years old. The author of the book of 2 Kings considered Josiah Judah's most outstanding king (2 Kings 23:25).

Don't Speak Evil about Anyone

△ ● ■ △ ○ ■ △ ● ■

BIBLE VERSE

Speak no evil about anyone . . .

Titus 3:2

Thoughts to Grow On:

"If you can't say something nice, don't say anything at all." This is a good course to follow *especially* when it comes to *people*.

This doesn't mean to keep silent when people *do* evil things. (That is a very *different* situation, and you can often be of great help *by* speaking up.) Instead, it means that you shouldn't set out to ruin someone's reputation, or cause others not to like someone.

Think about it. Would you like it if someone said ugly things about *you*?

Today:

Say only good things about people. Concentrate on their good qualities and share their good qualities with others.

🌐 MY AMAZING WORLD 🌐

While others saw only an uncontrollable, angry, deaf, blind, and mute (one who is not able to speak) little girl, Anne Sullivan saw a young lady who simply needed to learn how to communicate. Anne Sullivan's ability to focus on the good qualities of this little girl completely changed the child's life forever. This little girl grew up to become one of the most admired people who ever lived. The little girl's name? Helen Keller.

Faith Muscles

△ ● ■ △ ○ ◼ △ ○ ■

BIBLE VERSE

The Lord searches all the earth for people who
have given themselves completely to him. He wants
to make them strong.

2 CHRONICLES 16:9

Thoughts to Grow On:

If you exercised for ten minutes every day, your whole
body would become stronger. That's how it works with
your faith in God, too.

God is constantly watching you
to see when you obey him.
Each act of obedience to God
is like a workout session in
faith. God sees your obedience
and gives you new power that
strengthens your faith, which, in turn,
makes it easier to obey again.

But watch out! The opposite is true as well. If you hardly ever obey God, each temptation you have and every spiritual challenge you face will be more difficult to overcome.

Today:
Exercise your faith.

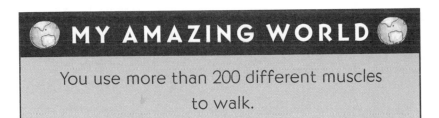

🌍 MY AMAZING WORLD 🌍

You use more than 200 different muscles to walk.

Capture Your Thoughts

We capture every thought and make it give up
and obey Christ.

2 CORINTHIANS 10:5

Thoughts to Grow On:

Can you stop a bad thought from
entering your brain? Maybe
sometimes, but you can *always*
decide what to do with that
thought. God says to *capture* it.
Take it as your prisoner and *make
it* obey God.

When you allow bad thoughts to
hang around, you give them the
power to destroy you. For
example, if you let a *jealous*

thought about someone make its home in your head, you might begin hating that person. Then, you'd have *two* bad thoughts hanging around—and on and on it goes.

God wants you to enjoy "life to the fullest." Bad thoughts seek to destroy your enjoyment of life.

Today:
Stand guard over your thoughts.

🌎 MY AMAZING WORLD 🌎

A spider uses sticky webs to catch its prey. Can a spider get caught in its own sticky web? Yes, but it usually doesn't because it weaves "non-sticky" threads, too. As long as the spider remembers how it built the web, it can avoid the sticky threads.

What Do I Wear?

△●□△○■△○□

BIBLE VERSE

"And don't worry about the clothes you
need for your body."

MATTHEW 6:25

Thoughts to Grow On:

Some people secretly fear that no one will like them
unless they look like a supermodel. How sad.

God wants you to be
smarter than that.
He wants you to
know that YOU are
his masterpiece. He
designed you more
marvelously than any
of his other creations.
He made you *in his
image.*

It doesn't matter whether you wear the most expensive clothes in town or garage-sale hand-me-downs—true beauty comes from God, *and it is yours already.*

Today:

If you're a girl, memorize Proverbs 31:30. If you're a boy, memorize Jeremiah 9:23–24.

 MY AMAZING WORLD

Italian painter Leonardo da Vinci's masterpiece the *Mona Lisa* was finished in 1503.
Today the painting is so valuable, it is considered "priceless."

I'm NOT Afraid

△ ● ■ △ ○ ■ △ ● ■

BIBLE VERSE

Even if I walk through a very dark valley, I will not be afraid because you [God] are with me.

PSALM 23:4

Thoughts to Grow On:

Fear has a way of changing things. At night, a shadow turns into a creepy monster, the ticktock of the clock becomes a giant's footsteps, and your heart climbs into your throat. You freeze with fright. Your face turns pale. You feel powerless.

There's only one way out: You must turn fear into faith. How? By reminding yourself of

what you already know. Pray a "praise prayer" right then and there—aloud if you'd like. Tell God how much you appreciate his awesome power to protect you from all harm. Thank him for always being with you (even in the dark). And relax, so that you can think more clearly.

Today:

Memorize the Bible verse at the beginning of this devotional.

🌎 MY AMAZING WORLD 🌎

Goldfish will often turn from gold to white
if left in a darkened room.

Say Helpful Things

△ ⬤ ◼ △ ◯ ◼ △ ◯ ◼

BIBLE VERSE

When you talk, do not say harmful things.
But say what people need—words that will help
others become stronger.

EPHESIANS 4:29

Thoughts to Grow On:

Would you be encouraged
if someone called you
a dummy because you
accidentally poured salt
(instead of sugar) into the
mixing bowl? Not likely.
Would it help if
someone called you
butterfingers after you
fumbled on the game-
winning touchdown?
Of course not.

The saying "Sticks and stones may break my bones, but words will never hurt me" isn't true. Words can hurt, but they can also *heal*. Words can break a person down or *build a person up*.

God wants you to use your mouth to *help* others. Before you blab out something foolish, ask yourself: What would help me if it were me instead of them?

Today:
Speak positive, helpful things.

🌎 MY AMAZING WORLD 🌎

A baby has 270 to 300 bones—more than an adult's 206. The reason? As you grow up, some of your bones grow together. This is called fusion.

Control Yourself

BIBLE VERSE

You must not be ruled by the things your sinful self makes you want to do.

ROMANS 6:12

Thoughts to Grow On:

You can change the TV channel with the push of a button. You can lock and unlock car doors the same way. All you need is a remote control.

Some people let *themselves* be controlled in a similar way. By their *impulses*. They *want* something, so they take it. They *feel* something, so they do it. It's like they've given the devil the remote control to their *lives*, and all he has to do is aim and click.

Do you allow your feelings, whims, or urges to control you? Or do you think about what God would want you to do?

Today:

Let *God* have the remote control to your life.

🌎 MY AMAZING WORLD 🌎

Though remote controls seem a recent invention, Zenith developed the first wired remote-control in 1950. The first wireless remote-control—also created by Zenith—came along five years later. It was called the "flash-matic."

Digging a Pit

△●■△○■△○■

BIBLE VERSE

Whoever digs a deep trap for others will fall into
it himself. Whoever tries to roll a boulder over
others will be crushed by it.

PROVERBS 26:27

Thoughts to Grow On:

Have you ever noticed that every trap Wile E. Coyote
sets for the Roadrunner backfires on him?

The book of Esther tells
of a real-life "Wile E.
Coyote" named
Haman. Haman was
determined to get
rid of a man named
Mordecai but each
evil scheme failed.
Finally, Haman built a

tall platform to hang Mordecai from. Guess who was hanged from it instead? . . . Haman.

A person may get away with doing evil for a while, but it will eventually destroy him. That's why it is so foolish to try to "get even" with someone—*it will only hurt you more*. Instead, simply forgive them.

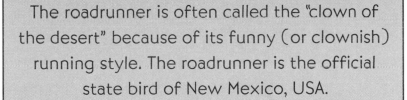

Today:
Begin reading the story of Esther.

MY AMAZING WORLD

The roadrunner is often called the "clown of the desert" because of its funny (or clownish) running style. The roadrunner is the official state bird of New Mexico, USA.

Discernment

△●■△○■△○■

BIBLE VERSE

"We are allowed to do all things." Yes. But all things
are not good for us to do.

1 CORINTHIANS 10:23

Thoughts to Grow On:

Do you know you can punch yourself in the nose? It's true, but it hurts! So, should you decide to do something simply because you are *able* to do it?

You have many freedoms and abilities. That's why you must develop *discernment and self-discipline. Discernment* means that you can determine whether something is right or wrong, helpful or harmful, wise or foolish. *Self-discipline* means that you can make yourself do the right thing—even when you're tempted to do the wrong thing.

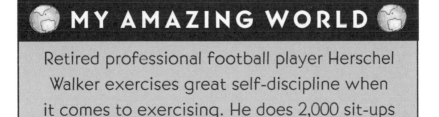

Discernment guides you. Self-discipline protects you. How do you get them? God teaches you as you follow him.

Today:

Use discernment and self-discipline three times today.

MY AMAZING WORLD

Retired professional football player Herschel Walker exercises great self-discipline when it comes to exercising. He does 2,000 sit-ups and 1,500 push-ups every day.

Honor Your Parents

△ ● ▢ △ ○ ▇ △ ● ▢

BIBLE VERSES

The command says, "Honor your father and mother."
This is the first command that has a promise with it.
The promise is: "Then everything will be well with you,
and you will have a long life on the earth."

EPHESIANS 6:2–3

Thoughts to Grow On:

Who gives you a place to live? Your parents. Who makes sure you have clothes to wear? Your parents. Who provides you with food; teaches you to make good choices; helps you when you're hurt; and cheers you up when you're sad? Your parents.

Your parents do all these things (and more!) because

they love you. God says you should not only obey them— you should *honor* them, too.

How do you *honor* them? By treating them as if they were the most important people in the world. By talking in a kind voice with kind words; by obeying their rules even when you're at a friend's house; by being proud of them.

Today:
If you haven't started honoring your parents already— start today.

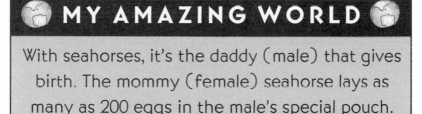

MY AMAZING WORLD

With seahorses, it's the daddy (male) that gives birth. The mommy (female) seahorse lays as many as 200 eggs in the male's special pouch. Four weeks later, they're the proud parents of about 200 tiny baby seahorses.

Be an Inspiration!

Let us think about each other and help each other to show love and do good deeds.

HEBREWS 10:24

Thoughts to Grow On:

It's easier to do good deeds and be excited about serving Jesus when everything is moving along smoothly. But what happens when the road gets bumpy? That's when people get frustrated, or become discouraged and want to throw in the towel.

But YOU can make a difference. YOU can be an

 inspiration and help turn a discouraged friend around. How? By listening to them—maybe they simply need to know that someone cares. Or, you can pray for them, send them a card, or tell them how much they've been an inspiration to you. The main thing is to *do something*.

Today:

Look around. Do you see any friends who need cheering up? Do it!

 MY AMAZING WORLD

Did you know that petting a dog can make you live longer? Studies have shown that petting an animal lowers your blood pressure; relieves loneliness, boredom, depression; and encourages laughter—the world's greatest medicine of all.

Be Happy-hearted

△ ◉ ▢ △ ○ ◼ △ ○ ▢

BIBLE VERSE

A happy heart is like good medicine. But a broken spirit drains your strength.

PROVERBS 17:22

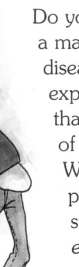

Thoughts to Grow On:

Do you know that there is a man who was cured of a disease by *laughing*? Medical experts recently discovered that laughing is a source of healing for the body. When you laugh, your body produces pain-relieving substances called *endorphins*. These endorphins help fight disease.

Here's more good news: You don't have to wait around until you *feel* happy—you can simply *choose* to be happy. You can make this choice in any situation, at any time. Not only will it improve your health, choosing a happy attitude will make even the least appealing chore a pleasant experience.

Today:

Choose to be happy.

MY AMAZING WORLD

You can enjoy the sunshine for 20 hours on a typical summer day in Alaska.

You're Not Too Young

△◐■△○■△●□

BIBLE VERSE

"You are young, but do not let anyone treat you as if you were not important. Be an example to show the believers how they should live."

1 TIMOTHY 4:12

Thoughts to Grow On:

In a lot of ways, it's a "grown-up's world." It may sometimes seem that this makes children less important. But guess what? Jesus told a group of grown-ups to become like *children*. And the verse above tells you how to turn your world around *while you're still young.*

Here's how you can be an example for grown-ups to learn from:

- Live for God.
- Honor God with the things you say.
- Share the love of God with others.
- Tell others about Jesus.
- Keep away from evil.

Today:
Do these things and you will win the hearts of the grown-ups in your world—*and inspire them to do better, too.*

🌎 MY AMAZING WORLD 🌎

Snowflakes—often thought of as tiny—have been recorded to be as big as 15 inches across and eight inches thick.

Pick Friends Wisely

△⬤◻△◯■△◯◻

| BIBLE VERSE |

Do not be fooled: "Bad friends will ruin good habits."

1 CORINTHIANS 15:33

Thoughts to Grow On:

Do you choose your friends or do you let your friends choose you? There's a big difference between these two approaches.

If you choose your friends, then you're on the right track. The next question is: How do you choose your friends? Do you choose them out of convenience—just because they live close by? Or, do you choose them because you like the same things?

God wants you to enjoy the best of friendships. That's why he tells you to choose your friends *wisely*. If you don't—or if you let your friends choose you—you may end up headed down the road to ruin.

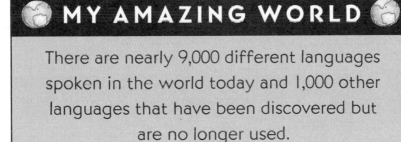

Today:

Think about the friendships in your life.

🌏 MY AMAZING WORLD 🌏

There are nearly 9,000 different languages spoken in the world today and 1,000 other languages that have been discovered but are no longer used.

Keep Moving Ahead

△ ● ▢ △ ○ ◼ △ ● ▢

BIBLE VERSES

But there is one thing I always do: I forget the things that are past. I try as hard as I can to reach the goal that is before me. I keep trying to reach the goal and get the prize.

PHILIPPIANS 3:13–14

Thoughts to Grow On:

Do you remember learning to ride a bike? You had to keep trying until you could maintain your balance *and* pedal *and* steer—all at the same time. You had an *exciting* goal in mind, and a few bruises and scratches weren't going to keep you from reaching it.

The same is true as you grow with Jesus. You will make mistakes along the way. You will get a "spiritual bruise" or two. That's how growing works. The important thing is to keep your eyes fixed on your goal of growing with Jesus.

Today:

Celebrate your victories.

 MY AMAZING WORLD

Bamboo can grow three feet taller in one day.

Overcome Evil with Good

△ ⬮ ◻ ◿ ◯ ◼ ◿ ◯ ◻

BIBLE VERSE

Do not let evil defeat you. Defeat evil by doing good.

ROMANS 12:21

Thoughts to Grow On:

Have you ever stood up for the right thing when others were trying to get you to do the wrong thing? Many times this is all it takes to turn the whole thing around, because *good will always defeat evil* just as light always overcomes darkness.

Try this sometime: Get a flashlight then turn off all the lights. Take a moment to notice how dark it is. Then turn on your flashlight.

The beam from the flashlight will overcome the darkness *immediately*. Look closely, you will *never* see the darkness smothering the light. The light is too strong.

Today:

Be a light for Jesus today. Take a stand against evil.

MY AMAZING WORLD

Light travels at 186,000 miles per second.

I Can Do All Things

△●■▲○■▲●■

BIBLE VERSE

I can do all things through Christ because he
gives me strength.

PHILIPPIANS 4:13

Thoughts to Grow On:

The apostle Paul had a rough
life. He was put in prison
many times because
of his faith in Jesus. He was
beaten, whipped, and struck
with rods. He was stoned and
left for dead. He survived three
shipwrecks—once spending
two days in the sea—and was
bitten by a poisonous snake.
He went hungry often and
nearly froze during the
winters.

Many people would've given up. Paul didn't. Instead, Paul *depended* on Jesus to give him the strength to make it through any challenge or hardship. God will give you strength, too.

Today:

Are you going through a tough time today? Lean on God.

 MY AMAZING WORLD

The poison in a black widow spider's bite is 15 times more deadly than the poison in a rattlesnake's bite.

Be Faithful in the Little Things

△ ● ■ △ ○ ■ △ ● ■

BIBLE VERSE

"You did well with small things. So I will let you care for much greater things. Come and share my happiness with me."

MATTHEW 25:21

Thoughts to Grow On:

Have you ever been given an important job? Maybe your mom asked you to watch your baby sister for a minute, or maybe your dad asked you to help him mend the fence. These types of tasks give you the opportunity to show your parents that you can handle big responsibilities.

When your parents see that you can handle these tasks, they are then able to give you even bigger responsibilities. Learning to be responsible is one of the most important things you'll master on your road to being a grown-up.

Today:

Think of something you can do to show your mom or dad that you can handle responsibility.

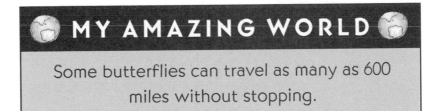

MY AMAZING WORLD

Some butterflies can travel as many as 600 miles without stopping.

Do Your Good Deeds in Secret

△●■△○■△○■

BIBLE VERSE

"Your giving should be done in secret. Your Father can see what is done in secret, and he will reward you."

MATTHEW 6:4

Thoughts to Grow On:

Guess what? God has given you a way to be sneaky and do the *right* thing at the same time. In fact, he's very much on the lookout to catch you every time you quietly do the right thing. Why? So he can *reward* you.

Don't do good things like a show-off. Instead, do good things for others *secretly*. Do good

because it pleases God and is truly kind and helpful. And don't worry if nobody thanks you or tells you how great you are. Remember this: God will never forget the good deeds you do—*and he sees every one.*

Today:
Secretly do a good deed for someone.

MY AMAZING WORLD

The South African wolf spider has a total of eight eyes, allowing it to see in all directions at once.

Be Quick to Listen

△ ● ▢ △ ○ ■ △ ○ ▢

BIBLE VERSE

My dear brothers, always be willing to listen. . . .

JAMES 1:19

Thoughts to Grow On:

Ask a partner to choose a short book to read aloud to you. *(Don't look at the book your partner has chosen.)* Now you choose a book to read to your partner. *(Don't let your partner see the book you've chosen.)* Begin reading aloud to one another—at the same time—on the count of three.

Did you learn much about each other's story?

Now, let your partner tell you about his or her

story while you listen. Then, switch roles, and you tell your partner about your story.

Did you learn much about each other's story this time?

Congratulations! You've just discovered a secret to being able to listen well—close your mouth.

Today:
Be a good listener.

MY AMAZING WORLD

Neither crickets nor spiders have ears. Instead, they have membranes that work like "sounding boards" located on their legs.

Stand Strong

△◑▢△○◙△○▢

BIBLE VERSE

When a person is tempted and still continues strong,
he should be happy.

JAMES 1:12

Thoughts to Grow On:

Have you ever wanted to do something you knew
you shouldn't do? That's called *temptation*.

Some temptations are
easy to say no to;
other ones seem to
never give up until you
give in. You're in a
spiritual tug-of-war.

Jesus knows all about your
struggles. He was tempted, too.
He will help you be strong if
you'll let him. And when you

win, be happy! You will have grown in your faith!
What if you fail? God will forgive you and give you
power to fight the next time.

Today:
Stand strong against
temptation.

🌎 MY AMAZING WORLD 🌎

Jim Abbott, a professional baseball pitcher
for the Milwaukee Brewers, overcame
incredible odds on his way to the big leagues.
His fastball has been clocked at 93 mph;
he won the 1998 Sullivan Award for being the
nation's top athlete; and he has even pitched
a no-hitter! Impressive? Here's the clincher—
Jim Abbott has only one hand.

You're Awesome!

△⬤◻️△⭕◼️△⭕◻️

BIBLE VERSE

"Say to God, 'Your works are amazing!'"

PSALM 66:3

Thoughts to Grow On:

Have you ever been complimented for something you did? Maybe you're an artist who amazes all your friends with your incredible drawings. Maybe you're the best speller in class, or the best helper a mom could imagine.

You do these things because you enjoy them. Still, it's wonderful when someone takes notice and says, "You're amazing!"

Guess what? When God hears his children tell him, "You're amazing, God!" he thinks it's wonderful, too.

Today:

Take time to brag on God today. Look around and admire his handiwork. Then stare into heaven and shout, "You're amazing, God!"

🌍 MY AMAZING WORLD 🌍

Astronomers estimate that there are 100 billion stars in our own galaxy—and that there may be 100 billion galaxies in the universe. Think about it: God knows each star by its name!

Can You Keep a Secret?

△◑◼△○◼△○◻

BIBLE VERSE

A trustworthy person can keep a secret.

PROVERBS 11:13

Thoughts to Grow On:

Good secrets should be kept. Here are some ways to determine if it is a good secret. Ask yourself:

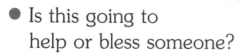

- Is this going to help or bless someone?
- Is this respecting someone's privacy?
- Is it something my parents would approve of?
- Is it something Jesus would approve of?

Here are some ways to determine if it is a bad secret. Ask yourself:

- Is it something that makes me feel ashamed, dirty, or frightened?
- Is it something I know I shouldn't be hearing about?
- Is it an unkind thing about someone else?
- Is someone's life in danger?
- Is someone about to be hurt?

Today:
Always keep good secrets. Have no part in keeping bad secrets.

🌍 MY AMAZING WORLD 🌍

The bat uses its hearing—not sight—to find food in the dark. It sends forth as many as 200 high-pitched "squeaks" per second. The "waves" from these sounds echo off the insects back to the bat.

Give Your Worries to God

△ ◉ ▢ △ ○ ▣ △ ○ ▢

BIBLE VERSE

Give all your worries to him, because he cares for you.

1 PETER 5:7

Thoughts to Grow On:

Are you worried about anything these days? Do you fear something might not turn out the way you'd like it to? Are you anxious? If so, God has good news for you—he'd like to take those worries off your mind and place them on his shoulders.

You can do this with a simple prayer. Tell God

what's on your mind. He has promised to listen and to care. You may want to talk with a Christian friend about things, too. Then both of you can pray about it together.

Today:

Worrying wears you down. God wants to lift you up. Tell God what's on your mind today.

🌎 MY AMAZING WORLD 🌎

You grow almost half an inch taller every night but shrink back the next day.

Think Good Thoughts

△●◻△○◼△●◻

Brothers, continue to think about the things that are good and worthy of praise. Think about the things that are true and honorable and right and pure and beautiful and respected.

PHILIPPIANS 4:8

Thoughts to Grow On:

Did you know that everyone wears glasses? Oh, you can't always see them. These are the glasses through which you see the world, yourself, events, and others.

Some wear *distrusting* glasses. Some wear *bitter* glasses. Others wear *party* glasses—they see life

as one big party where
they can behave wildly.
Others wear *I'm-better-
than-everyone-else* glasses

(these, by the way, make you blind to all the
wonderfully fascinating people you might've gotten
to know).

God says, "Wear *love, praise, and purity* glasses."
These will help you "see" (experience) things from an
attitude of love, praise for God, purity, and truth.

Today:
See for yourself what type of glasses you wear.

🌍 MY AMAZING WORLD 🌍

Each of your eyes is made up of around 130
million light-sensitive cells.

Respect Others

△ ● ■ △ ○ ■ △ ● ■

BIBLE VERSE

Show respect for all people.

1 PETER 2:17

Thoughts to Grow On:

The Bible never says you have to like everyone—it says you have to love them. This kind of love isn't something you *feel* (at least, not every time); it's something you *do*—simply because you have made a *choice* to do it.

This is why you can show respect for someone you don't *like*. You can treat them with kindness and patience—not because you enjoy hanging out with them, but because they, too, are made in the image of God.

Remember:

- Be considerate of their feelings—even if they aren't considerate of yours.
- Be kind—even if they're mean to you.
- Love them—even if they're hateful to you.

Today:

Say a prayer for someone you don't like.

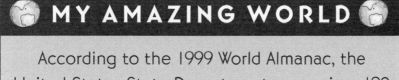

MY AMAZING WORLD

According to the 1999 World Almanac, the United States State Department recognizes 190 independent states (countries) in the world.

Armor of God

△ ● ▪ △ ○ ▪ △ ● ▪

Wear the full armor of God. Wear God's armor so that you can fight against the devil's evil tricks.

EPHESIANS 6:11

Thoughts to Grow On:

Clothes are not only for looks, they also have *functions*. A heavy coat keeps you warm in the winter. A football uniform is padded to keep you from getting hurt (it doesn't always work). A smock helps keep you from getting paint on your clothes.

God has a set of clothes you should wear every

day. Actually, it is armor. Why do you need to wear armor? The same reason the knights of long ago wore it—to protect you in battle. And YOU, child of God, are in a battle against the devil.

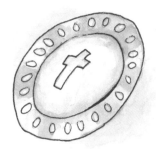

Today:
Read Ephesians 6:10–17. Think about each item of clothing it mentions.

Your hair may be thought of as part of your body's armor. Hair helps protect your skin from the sun's harsh rays and provides additional insulation from the cold. Eyelashes help keep dust and other harmful particles out of your eyes. A typical child's head has around 75,000 hairs on it. An eyelash hair will only last about 150 days. A head hair may last between two and four years.

The Spirit Gives *Love*

But the Spirit gives love, . . .

GALATIANS 5:22

Thoughts to Grow On:

Love means having a special feeling of affection for someone or something. You can *love* your pet. You can *love* spaghetti. You can *love* your family. But do you have the same kind of love for your family that you have for spaghetti? No way!

This verse is talking about a special kind of love. It's called *agapé* (pronounced *ah•gah•pay*) love. Agapé love is God's love. It is a *perfect love* he has for every person.

Agapé love gives you the power and desire to love *even your enemies*. God has given you agape love—his own love—as a gift.

Today:
Use agapé love.

Don't Lie

△●■△○■△○■

BIBLE VERSE

Do not lie to each other. . . .

COLOSSIANS 3:9

Thoughts to Grow On:

When you lie, you are teaching others not to believe you. You are treating others as fools. It's like you are secretly convinced that they will never be smart enough to "find you out." Worse still, you will have to tell more lies to cover the first lie.

Worst of all, when you lie, you are *destroying yourself* from the inside out. No one can be *truly* happy and be a liar at the same time. It's impossible. You can't be truly happy when you can't respect yourself.

Lying may get you out of something *for the moment*, but it will turn on you in the end.

Today:
Tell the truth.

The Spirit Gives *Gentleness*

△●▢△○■△○▢

BIBLE VERSES

But the Spirit gives . . . gentleness . . .
GALATIANS 5:22–23

Thoughts to Grow On:

There is a 1,000-year-old fable about an argument between the wind and the sun. Each thought it could get a man to take off his coat more quickly than the other.

The wind blew hard against the man, but the man pulled his coat even more tightly around himself. Exasperated, the wind gave up. The sun then heated

124

itself, gently warming the day.
Soon, the man took off his coat.

This is a story about *gentleness.*
Often when you try to *force*
someone to do something,
they will struggle against doing it.
However, if you use *gentleness,* they will happily
agree to do it.

Today:
Approach things with *gentleness.*

MY AMAZING WORLD

A tornado's winds can reach a speed of
almost 300 miles per hour!

Be Humble

BIBLE VERSE

When you do things, do not let selfishness or pride be
your guide. Be humble and give more honor to others
than to yourselves.

PHILIPPIANS 2:3

Thoughts to Grow On:

You've probably heard
someone say, "Don't be a
sore loser," but have you
ever heard, "Don't be a sore
winner"?

It's thrilling to be the winner,
but it is something you
should celebrate with a
humble attitude. Sore
winners brag and gloat.
Humble winners are
excited to have won, but

they don't get a "big head" about it. They know that having a winning *attitude* is more important than having a winning score.

Being humble means not to think more highly of yourself than you should. God made each person in a marvelously incredible way— and no one is more valuable than another.

Today:
Choose a humble, helpful attitude.

MY AMAZING WORLD

In Greek mythology a fable is told of a handsome young man named Narcissus who saw his reflection in a pool of water and immediately fell madly in love with himself. He was so captivated by his own image that he sat and stared at it until he died.

Be Considerate

△ ● ■ △ ○ ■ △ ○ ■

BIBLE VERSE

Do not be interested only in your own life, but be interested in the lives of others.

PHILIPPIANS 2:4

Thoughts to Grow On:

Here are seven ways to show consideration for others:

1. Say "Thank you" when others help you.
2. Let your guest decide which game to play first.
3. Give the biggest ice cream cone to someone else.
4. Play quietly while someone else is on the phone.

5. Put things back when you've finished using them.

6. Take special care of borrowed things, and return them quickly.

7. Be a good listener.

Being considerate means behaving in ways that show you care about others' feelings. It starts when you choose to pay attention to what *others* are experiencing, talking about, or going through.

Today:
Be considerate of others.

MY AMAZING WORLD

During a drought, the Helmet frog uses its head as the door to its house. This keeps moisture in so it (and the other frogs with it) can live.

The Spirit Gives Joy

△ ● ■ ◢ ○ ■ ◢ ○ ■

BIBLE VERSE

But the Spirit gives . . . joy . . .

GALATIANS 5:22

Thoughts to Grow On:

Think of something that makes you especially happy. Is it a puppy licking your face? Wrestling with your dad? Waking up on Christmas morning? Close your *eyes* for a minute and *capture* that memory or experience before you read any further.

Do you still have some of that feeling left even when your eyes are open? That feeling is called *joy*. Joy goes beyond happiness to *delight*. Lots of things can *make* you happy—truly special things *give* you joy. Today's verse says that God's Holy Spirit *gives* joy for your delight (Galatians 5:22).

Today:

Take a few minutes to think about God's love for you. As you do so, you will experience his joy.

MY AMAZING WORLD

The laughing hyena can grow to a length of 6 feet and weigh as much as 180 pounds.

Show Respect to Others

△⬤⬛△◯⬛△◯⬛

BIBLE VERSE

Do not speak angrily to an older man, but talk to him as if he were your father. Treat younger men like brothers. Treat older women like mothers, and younger women like sisters.

1 TIMOTHY 5:1

Thoughts to Grow On:
Why did God give you a mouth? Sure, you need it to eat with, but why did he make it *talk*? Did he make it for ugly talk? Did he make it for sassy talk? No, of course not. Then why did God make us able to talk? So that we could *understand* one another.

How would you feel if someone took your favorite toy or possession and misused it? When you use your mouth to be ugly, sassy, cruel, or destructive, you are *misusing* one of your most valuable possessions. Instead, use your mouth as a tool in God's hand— to love, to inspire, to encourage, to bless.

Today:
Use your mouth for good.

MY AMAZING WORLD

Flies are able to taste with their feet.

Don't Overstay Your Welcome

△ ⬤ ◻ △ ◯ ◼ △ ◯ ◻

BIBLE VERSE

Don't go to your neighbor's house too often.
Too much of you will make him hate you.

PROVERBS 25:17

Thoughts to Grow On:

Have you ever had a friend spend a few days or a week with you? The first day or so was probably a total blast, but by the third or fourth day, you may have started getting on each other's nerves.

Does this mean you don't like each other anymore? Not at all. It simply means you need to spend some time away from each other. That's part of being best friends, too.

God made people to enjoy—and *need*—good friendships, but even the best friendships will not fill your spirit fully. You need to spend time alone with God for that.

Today:
Enjoy your friends today, but enjoy God more.

🌍 MY AMAZING WORLD 🌍

Beavers may come home to visit, but they must live at least one mile away after they are a year old.

Work Steadily

△◑■△◯■△◯■

BIBLE VERSE

Do not be lazy but work hard.

ROMANS 12:11

Thoughts to Grow On:

Do you remember the story of the hard-working ant and the lazy grasshopper? The ant worked hard all summer storing up for the winter while the grasshopper played.

You may not need to worry about food for the winter, but you do have work to do. Chores, schoolwork, piano lessons, karate, Bible study—these require work if you're going to do them well. If you do only enough to "get by," you won't be much better off than the grasshopper. And even what little you master may be forgotten so quickly, it will be as if you never learned it.

Today:
Work diligently* at your tasks.

Piano Recital Today

🌍 MY AMAZING WORLD 🌍

Pacific salmon travel as many as 1,000 miles—often upstream—scaling waterfalls ten feet high on their final journey home.

---

* New word? *Diligent(ly)* means steadily, with a focused effort, and with great care.

God Never Sleeps

△ ● ■ △ ○ ■ △ ● ■

He who guards you never sleeps.

PSALM 121:3

Thoughts to Grow On:

A very insightful four-year-old told his father that God doesn't have a bed. His father asked how he knew this. The child answered, "Because God never sleeps." Oh! What a wonderful truth! You can go to God any time, *day or night*, and *he is always there!*

Are you having a bad morning? Tell God about it. Are things going rough at school?

Talk to God! Did your mom make your favorite dish for dinner? Share your joy with Jesus. Did a nightmare wake you up in the middle of the night? Jesus is right there, ready to give you his peace.

Today:

Hey, guess what? You can talk to God *right now*.

 MY AMAZING WORLD

Without enough sleep, your body is more likely to become sick. Sleep allows your body to repair and rebuild and grow.

God Knows Everything

△●■△○■△○□

BIBLE VERSE

God knows everything people do, even the things done in secret.

ECCLESIASTES 12:14

Thoughts to Grow On:

Have you ever played the game hide-and-seek? It's a lot of fun, but no matter how good you are at hiding, you can't hide from God. Adam and Eve tried this very thing in the garden but, of course, it didn't work.

God doesn't watch you all the time so that he can write down every bad thing you do.

Instead, he watches over you with the love and care of the good shepherd who eagerly takes care of his sheep (that's *you*). He wants to keep you from harm, lead you beside still waters, and take you into green pastures. Simply put, God wants to give you the best!

Today:

Know that God is with you.

 MY AMAZING WORLD

Ostriches hide by sitting with their heads and necks stretched out on the ground. Some ostriches have grown as tall as eight feet, and have weighed as much as 300 pounds. Amazingly, ostriches can run faster than horses.

Jesus Comforts You

△●□△○■△●□

BIBLE VERSE

"He has sent me to comfort all those who are sad."

ISAIAH 61:2

Thoughts to Grow On:

Sadness comes when you lose someone or something that you loved. Sadness comes when things don't work out the way you hoped they would—or, when you've been hoping for something and it doesn't happen at all.

Jesus is your best friend. He knows what it feels like to be sad. He was sad, too, when he was here on earth. He knows what it feels like to lose someone you love. He knows what it feels like to be deeply disappointed.

But he also knows the way *out* of sadness, and if you'll let him, he'll lead you out of yours, too.

Today:
Talk to Jesus about your sadness.

 MY AMAZING WORLD

When a person is nervous or upset, the body often releases more acid into the stomach, which, in turn, may cause damage to the stomach lining. Also, when you are unhappy, your heart will usually beat faster.

Do Not Insult Others

△ ◉ ▢ △ ○ ▣ △ ● ▢

BIBLE VERSE

Do not do wrong to a person to pay him back for
doing wrong to you. Or do not insult someone to pay
him back for insulting you. But ask God to bless that
person. Do this, because you yourselves were called
to receive a blessing.

1 PETER 3:9

Thoughts to Grow On:

Has someone made fun of
you? Has anyone ever
called you a mean name?
Said something ugly about
you behind your back?

People made fun of Jesus.
They called him ugly names
and treated him horribly. They
shouted one insult after another.

Do you know what Jesus did about it? He blessed them and asked God to forgive them.

When people hurt you with their words, don't yell insults back at them. Do what Jesus did—forgive and bless them. Why? So you'll get a blessing yourself. God will see to that.

Today:

Remember to act as Jesus did when troublemakers come your way.

🌏 MY AMAZING WORLD 🌏

Gorillas usually stick out their tongues when they are angry at you.

Do Not Steal

△●■△○■△●■

If a person is stealing, he must stop stealing. . . .

Ephesians 4:28

Thoughts to Grow On:

If you've ever had something stolen from you, you know how horrible it feels to be "ripped off." You feel angry, invaded, and violated. It can also leave you feeling anxious and wondering if you might be stolen from again. This is a big part of why God says not to steal from others. He knows how devastating it can be to those who have been robbed—even if it's just a "little thing" that was stolen.

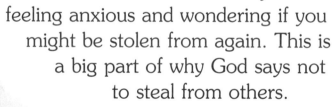

But there are other reasons not to steal:

- It's *dishonest*.
- It isn't *fair*.
- It often *leads to other evil behaviors*.
- It *dishonors God*.

Today:

If you're tempted to steal today, ask God to help you.

 MY AMAZING WORLD

An insect that has been robbed of its head can live for as long as a year without it.

Obey When Nobody Sees

△●▢△○▣△○▢

BIBLE VERSE

You obeyed God when I was with you. It is even more important that you obey now while I am not with you.

PHILIPPIANS 2:12

Thoughts to Grow On:

When you were little, you had to obey your parents whether you wanted to or not. Why? Because they were always watching you to make sure you were safe, and if you misbehaved they were right there to correct you.

You're older now, and often do activities away from your parents. How are you handling that? Are you obeying and honoring your parents even though they can't see you? If so, you are also honoring God—and yourself! You are showing the

 world that you truly love your parents, and that you are growing up to be a respectful and trustworthy young person.

Today:

Honor your parents while you're away from them (and while you're with them).

 MY AMAZING WORLD

Baby scorpions travel by lying on their mommies' backs until they are two weeks old. Then they can walk all by themselves.

Jesus Is the Son of God

△ ● ▢ ⬜ △ ○ ▢ ⬛ △ ● ▢

BIBLE VERSE

Simon Peter answered, "You are the Christ, the Son of the living God."

MATTHEW 16:16

Thoughts to Grow On:

The apostle Peter said something incredible about Jesus. It was something he would never say about any other person who would *ever* live. He said that his *friend*, Jesus, was the long-awaited Savior of the world. He said that his *friend*, Jesus, was the Son of God himself.

Can you imagine saying this about one of your friends?

Peter couldn't *prove* it. It was something he *believed*. It was a statement of *faith*, and it totally changed his life.

That was thousands of years ago. Now Jesus is asking you the same question he asked Peter: "Who do you say that I am?"

Today:
Will you answer him today?

🌎 MY AMAZING WORLD 🌎

The owl butterfly frightens predators away by the two "owl eyes" designed into its wings. The predator thinks it is seeing an owl and leaves the butterfly alone.

Jesus Knocks on Your Heart

△ ● ■ △ ○ ■ △ ● ■

BIBLE VERSE

"Here I am! I stand at the door and knock. If anyone hears my voice and opens the door, I will come in and eat with him. And he will eat with me."

REVELATION 3:20

Thoughts to Grow On:

The Cat in the Hat is a made-up story about a cat who barges into two children's house while their parents are away. Much to the children's shock (and over the protests of the wise fish), the cat makes a total disaster of the children's house.

152

Jesus is knocking *in real life*. He's
knocking on the door of your heart.
He wouldn't think of barging in.
No, he waits for you to invite him in.
And, once you do, he will clean *every*
sin in your "spiritual house" with his love,
and make everything new.

Today:

Will you invite Jesus in today?

MY AMAZING WORLD

In ancient Egypt cats were considered to be
uniquely connected to the false "gods" the
Egyptians worshiped. When an Egyptian's cat
died, the owner shaved his (or her) eyebrows
off to show how sad he (or she) felt.

Christ Is the Passover Lamb

△●■△○■△●■

BIBLE VERSE

For Christ, our Passover lamb, was killed to cleanse us.

1 CORINTHIANS 5:7

Thoughts to Grow On:

Do you remember the story of the ten plagues? First, God turned water into blood. Then God covered the land with frogs! The last plague was the worst. God had the death angel fly over the land and kill every firstborn son.

Only one thing would save a firstborn son

that night. God told the Israelites to kill a lamb and paint its blood over the doorposts of their homes. When the death angel saw the blood, it let the firstborn son inside that house live. This night is called "Passover," because the angel "passed over" the houses.

Jesus is your Passover lamb. This means that God has "passed over" your sins because of Jesus' blood.

Today:
Praise God for this wonderful miracle.

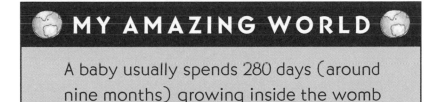

MY AMAZING WORLD

A baby usually spends 280 days (around nine months) growing inside the womb before being born.

Don't Talk Too Much

BIBLE VERSE

There is a time to be silent and a time to speak.

ECCLESIASTES 3:7

Thoughts to Grow On:

You know to be quiet:

- during class at school (unless your teacher calls on you)
- at bedtime (after all the kisses, prayers, and giggles)
- while someone else is talking

Here are some other times worth trying out:

- in the early morning (listen to the birds)
- when you're praying (sometimes you need to listen)
- when you're beside a stream (very nice)
- when you don't really have anything to say (in other words, don't talk just to be talking)
- when someone needs a shoulder to cry on (be a friend)

Silence can be a wonderful thing.

Today:
Try to be quiet more than you talk.

MY AMAZING WORLD

The German composer Ludwig van Beethoven is considered to be one of the greatest musical composers of all time. Some of his most impressive compositions were written *after* he went completely deaf in 1817.

Peace in God's Family

△ ● ■ △ ○ ■ △ ○ ■

BIBLE VERSE

It is good and pleasant when God's people
live together in peace!

PSALM 133:1

Thoughts to Grow On:

If you have a brother or
sister, you know that
sometimes you have
conflicts. The question
is: What happens next?
Do the conflicts lead to
pushing, shoving, or
calling each other names?
Do they lead to bitter feelings?

The Bible gives us two pairs of
brothers to learn from: Cain and
Abel; and Jacob and Esau.

Cain became jealous of Abel. Cain let his jealousy grow into bitter feelings that led to anger. In the end, he killed Abel.

Jacob tricked Esau out of his blessing. This broke Esau's heart. In the end, they forgave each other and found peace again.

Today:
Strive for peace with your family members.

 MY AMAZING WORLD

Talk about poor family relationships! The black widow spider got its name because the female kills and eats the male after mating.

God Loves Us All the Same

△ ● ▢ △ ◯ ■ △ ● ▢

BIBLE VERSE

"God is not better to princes than other people. He is not better to rich people than poor people. This is because he made them all with his own hands."

JOB 34:19

Thoughts to Grow On:
Are you the fastest runner in your school? No? That's okay. God loves you just the same. Are you the smartest kid in your school? No? That's okay, too. God loves you just as much as he loves anyone else.

You don't have to be the brightest, the funniest, the tallest, the strongest, the bravest, or the most talented before God will love you.

And if you happen to be the brightest, funniest, strongest, bravest, or most talented person in the world, it won't make God love you more.

God loves everyone the same. He has no favorites.

There is no competition for God's love—there's plenty for everyone!

Today:
Enjoy God's love for you.

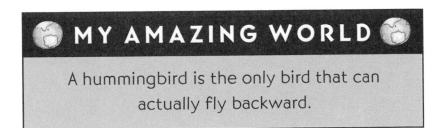

🌍 MY AMAZING WORLD 🌍

A hummingbird is the only bird that can actually fly backward.

You Are the Light of the World

△ ● ■ △ ○ ■ △ ○ ■

BIBLE VERSE

"You are the light that gives light to the world. . . ."

MATTHEW 5:14

Thoughts to Grow On:

Imagine you are on a hiking trip with your friends, and you don't make it back to camp before dark. Everyone is nervous and frozen in fear.

Now imagine you could snap your fingers and make a flashlight appear instantly. You'd be the hero of the day! Everyone would follow your every step.

162

Guess what? That's the way it is in your real world.
Without Jesus, people live in *spiritual* darkness.
They can't see where to go.
If you love Jesus, you have the
light of his power, wisdom, and
love to guide others to God.

Today:
Let your light shine so that
others can see the way to Jesus.

MY AMAZING WORLD

Our sun gives light to the whole world, and yet
it is 93 million miles away from the earth.

Inspire Others to Praise God

△●■△○■△○■

BIBLE VERSE

Lord, let me live so people will praise you.

PSALM 143:11

Thoughts to Grow On:

Have you ever seen a line of dominoes being toppled over one by one? People have set up huge and amazing domino designs where thousands of dominoes bump into one another until all of them have fallen over.

Some call this the "domino effect." It means that a certain *action* will

"domino" or "lead to" a certain *result*.

God wants you to use your daily life as a *domino effect* for his glory. God knows that your good behavior will lead to someone else's good behavior. Your obedience to God will "domino" into inspiring someone else to obey and please God.

Today:
Be a "Jesus domino."

🌍 MY AMAZING WORLD 🌍

Your body has "domino-effect digestion."
Take a bite of something, and immediately
saliva is squirted on it from under your tongue.
Once wet, it can slip down into your stomach.
Every day, your body produces about three
pints of saliva—enough to fill four soda cans.

The Walking Bible

△⬤▢△◯◼△⬤▢

BIBLE VERSE

You yourselves are our letter, written on our hearts. It is known and read by everyone.

2 CORINTHIANS 3:2

Thoughts to Grow On:

Have you ever seen someone using sign language? Sign language is a language "spoken" with your hands. People who cannot hear "read" the signer's hands in order to understand what is being communicated.

God wants you to know that your *life* is also a language that people read every day. People watch the way you behave, they listen to the things you say and *how*

GOD

LOVES

ME!

you say them, and they determine what kind of person you are.

God wants you to be a *walking* Bible. He wants you to live your life obeying his Word so that others will learn how great God is by *reading* YOU.

I LOVE YOU

Today:
Be a walking Bible.

MY AMAZING WORLD

Moths do not use their ears or sign language to listen. Instead, they hear through hairs on their body.

Be Dependable

△ ● ▢ △ ○ ■ △ ● ▢

"You must do whatever you say you will do."

DEUTERONOMY 23:23

Thoughts to Grow On:

Jesus told a story about a man with two sons. He asked each son to help him work. The first son said, "Sorry, Dad, but I can't help you today." The second son quickly agreed to help. "Sure, Dad!" he said. "You can count on me!"

As things turned out, the second son didn't show up. Thankfully, the first son changed his mind and rushed out to help.

How do you feel when someone "breaks" their word to you? Is it smart to depend on someone who doesn't keep his promises?

Today:
If you say you'll do something, be sure and really do it.

Be a Helper

△⬤▢◿◯▨◿◯▢

BIBLE VERSE

I know that you want to help.

2 CORINTHIANS 9:2

Thoughts to Grow On:

The book of Acts tells about a lady named Tabitha (you may know her as Dorcas). Tabitha was a very kind woman who loved God with all of her heart. Tabitha was a giver. The Bible says, "She was always doing good and helping the poor" (Acts 9:36).

You go first.

Sadly, she died, and many cried. Her friends sent for the apostle Peter. As soon as Peter arrived, people began showing him the different coats and shirts Tabitha had made for them while she was alive. Miraculously, God used Peter to bring Tabitha back to life.

Tabitha spent her life doing good things for others. God wants you to do the same.

Today:
Start doing good things for others.

 MY AMAZING WORLD

A queen honeybee lays up to 1,500 eggs per day. Some queen honeybees lay one million eggs in a lifetime, which means the queen may live only a year or two.

Be a Genius

BIBLE VERSE

The Lord's teachings are perfect . . .
They make plain people wise.

PSALM 19:7

Thoughts to Grow On:

Would you like to be brilliant without having to be the school's best speller? It's possible!

Would you like to be a genius without having to ace your science test? It's easy to achieve!

Certainly, you should always do your very best to learn all you can in school and in life, but true genius is a gift from God. However, it is a gift God gives to anyone who wants it.

All you need to do is learn and obey God's teachings. But God makes it even easier than that—he gives you the *desire* to learn his ways and the *power* to obey them!

Today:

Begin your studies as a "God-Scholar."

 MY AMAZING WORLD

Your brain weighs about 13 ounces when you're a baby, almost three pounds by your seventh birthday, and will be as heavy as it's ever going to be—usually a full three pounds (the weight of a large grapefruit)—when you're 20 years old.

Be Rich

△ ● ▢ △ ○ ▣ △ ● ▢

BIBLE VERSES

The Lord's judgments are true. . . . They are worth
more than gold, even the purest gold.

PSALM 19:9–10

Thoughts to Grow On:

It seems like everybody wants to
be rich. You see commercials on
TV about it; you hear songs
on the radio about it; and
every once in a while
you may even find a
large envelope in
your mailbox
claiming that
becoming rich is as
simple as mailing in
a reply card.

God has a better way to true riches than any of these. He wants to lead you to the treasure-box of riches he has buried in his Word. Each verse you read is a shovelful of the purest gold in the world. God's gold brings you a lifetime of riches, and it can never be stolen or ruined.

Today:

Start digging for God's treasures.

MY AMAZING WORLD

A squirrel hides 20 (or more) bushels of food each winter but rarely needs more than two bushels to survive until springtime.

God Forgives as You Forgive

△ ● ▢ △ ○ ■ △ ● ▢

BIBLE VERSES

"If you forgive others for the things they do wrong,
then your Father in heaven will also forgive you for the
things you do wrong. But if you don't forgive the
wrongs of others, then your Father in heaven will not
forgive the wrong things you do."

MATTHEW 6:14–15

Thoughts to Grow On:
Did you know that God's
forgiveness actually *stops*
when you refuse to forgive
others?

Your friendship with God is
possible because of his
forgiveness. If God were
unwilling to forgive your sins,

176

your sins would build an invisible wall between him and you. But God placed *every* sin you'd ever have on Jesus and washed them away at the cross. Forgiveness is important because it cost God the life of his very own Son.

Who do you need to forgive today? A friend? A schoolmate? Your mom or dad? Everyone makes mistakes. Sometimes these mistakes may hurt or disappoint you.

Today:
Don't build a wall of bitterness or anger around your heart. Instead, choose to forgive.

🌍 MY AMAZING WORLD 🌍

The Great Wall of China is 1,500 miles long, 25 feet tall, and 25 feet thick. The roadway on top of the wall is wide enough for 10 soldiers to walk side by side. It took 10 years to build it.

Life Can Be Hard

△ ◐ ▢ ◿ ◯ ▣ ◿ ◯ ▢

BIBLE VERSE

"But the gate that opens the way to true life is very small. And the road to true life is very hard. Only a few people find that road."

MATTHEW 7:14

Thoughts to Grow On:

Jesus says that your life's direction will be determined by two gates: a wide gate and a narrow gate. Although it may not seem like it at times, the wide gate leads to heartache, frustration, and trouble. The small gate leads to true life.

Jesus is warning you to be careful. Do not "walk through" the wide doors of sin and disobedience even when you see other people doing it. Instead, Jesus says, walk through the small gate. How? By obeying God.

It won't always be easy to do, but it will always lead to true life.

Today:
Follow God's path to true life with your choices today.

 MY AMAZING WORLD

It took 80,000 miles of wire cables and 80,000 tons of structural steel to build the Golden Gate Bridge.

Be a Servant

△ ◐ ▢ ◁ ○ ■ ◁ ○ ▢

BIBLE VERSE

So prepare your minds for service and
have self-control.

1 PETER 1:13

Thoughts to Grow On:

Even though Jesus is the Son of
God, he lived his life on earth
serving others. He once said that
he did not come *to be served*,
but to *serve* (Mark 10:45).

When you choose to serve
others instead of trying to get
them to do things for you,
you're behaving like Jesus.
Jesus said, "If one of
you wants to become the
most important, then he

must serve all of you like a slave" (Mark 10:44).

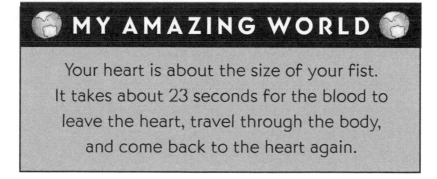

An example is Mother Teresa, who died in 1997. Although she was born into a comfortable lifestyle, she chose to leave that behind and spend her life quietly serving poor people. Many consider her one of the most important people of our time.

Today:
Make sure your heart is a "servant's heart." Find a way to do something kind for someone else.

🌐 MY AMAZING WORLD 🌐
Your heart is about the size of your fist. It takes about 23 seconds for the blood to leave the heart, travel through the body, and come back to the heart again.

God Will Make You Strong

△ ⬮ ◻ △ ○ ◼ △ ○ ◻

BIBLE VERSE

"I am sad and tired. Make me strong again as you have promised."

PSALM 119:28

Thoughts to Grow On:

Do you ever have days that completely wear you out? It's easy to feel discouraged and irritable on days like these, and to begin treating people badly.

God has an answer for these kinds of days: He'll make you strong. This doesn't mean you'll have huge arm muscles to flex. It means you'll have a new *inner* strength—new energy—to get you through your day.

Here are other things you can do that will help, too:

- Get a good rest at night (and nap sometimes).
- Exercise every day.
- Eat healthy food.

Today:
Tell God if you feel discouraged or exhausted. Ask him for his strength.

🌐 MY AMAZING WORLD 🌐

An adult kangaroo could jump from home plate to first base in a single leap.

Be a Jesus Volunteer

△◐▣▢△◯▢△◯▣

BIBLE VERSE

"Then I heard the Lord's voice. He said,
'Whom can I send? Who will go for us?' So I said,
'Here I am. Send me!'"

ISAIAH 6:8

Thoughts to Grow On:

Have you ever offered to do
something you didn't have to do?
If so, you were a *volunteer*.
Do you remember how satisfying
it felt to know you were doing a
good thing even though no one
was telling you to do it?

God is looking for volunteers. God
is looking for people who are eager
to obey him. He is looking for
people who will do what the

Old Testament prophet Isaiah did, and stand up and say, "Here I am. Send *me!*"

Today:

When you see an opportunity to serve the Lord today, step up and tell God, "Send *me*, Lord! Let *me* be the one to please you in this situation!" Then do the job *gladly*.

🌍 MY AMAZING WORLD 🌍

Over one million volunteers enable the Red Cross organization to help people all over the world. About 400,000 of these volunteers are 18 years old—or younger.

Be Like Jesus

BIBLE VERSE

"I did this as an example for you. So you should do
as I have done for you."

JOHN 13:15

Thoughts to Grow On:

Can you think of someone you really admire? Often
when people admire someone, they may secretly wish
to be like that person in
many ways. Some do
more than wish! They try
their hardest to look,
dress, talk, walk, and act
just like the person they
admire.

Jesus wants you to try
to copy him. He wants
you to do all you can to

talk, act, and think like him. As you read your
Bible, you'll learn what he was really like.
You'll discover how he spent his days
helping others and how he
forgave people when they
treated him unkindly.

Today:
Read John 13:3–17 to
learn more about Jesus.

MY AMAZING WORLD

The average child takes 19,000 steps per
day (give or take a few). This adds up to
nearly eight miles!

Jesus Always Accepts You

△ ◕ ■ ▲ △ ◯ ■ ▲ ◯ ■

BIBLE VERSE

"The Father gives me my people. Every one of them
will come to me, and I will always accept them."

JOHN 6:37

Thoughts to Grow On:

People can be downright mean sometimes. Some
people act like they think you're
great one minute and the
next minute treat you
like a fly at a picnic.

Some people refuse
to be friends with
someone if that
person doesn't wear
the *right* clothes, or
live in the *right*

neighborhood, or go to the *right* school. Sometimes it's for even sillier reasons than these (like not liking the *same* music or the *same* TV shows).

Jesus loves you no matter what and *just the way you are*. He will *never* reject you or be embarrassed to be your friend.

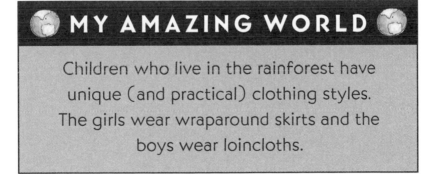

Today:
Spend time with your best friend, Jesus.

🌍 MY AMAZING WORLD 🌍

Children who live in the rainforest have unique (and practical) clothing styles. The girls wear wraparound skirts and the boys wear loincloths.

Jesus Is Your Shepherd

△ ⬤ ◻ △ ◯ ◼ △ ⬤ ◻

BIBLE VERSE

The Lord takes care of his people like a shepherd.
He gathers the people like lambs in his arms.
He carries them close to him. He gently leads
the mothers of the lambs.

ISAIAH 40:11

Thoughts to Grow On:
When God thinks of you,
he thinks of you as kindly
and tenderly as you might
think of a precious baby
lamb. He even describes
himself as our *shepherd*.

Shepherds are very
careful with their
sheep. They keep

their flock safe from hungry wolves. Jesus keeps us safe from the devil. Shepherds lead their sheep beside calm streams so they can drink. They lead them to the pastures where the grass is the greenest. And if a lamb wanders off, the shepherd leaves the other sheep to find the lost one.

Jesus is your shepherd. He watches over you with great love and care.

Today:
Rest in Jesus' love.

 MY AMAZING WORLD

"Mary Had a Little Lamb" is not only a popular nursery rhyme, in 1877 it became the first words of recorded human speech when Thomas Edison invented the phonograph (record player). By the way, the rhyme was written in 1830 by Mrs. Sarah Josepha Hale of Boston, who wrote the poem about a real girl named Mary and the lamb who actually followed her to school one day.

Tell God Your Sins

△ ◐ ▣ △ ○ ▢ △ ◐ ▢

BIBLE VERSE

But if we confess our sins, he will forgive our sins. We can trust God. He does what is right. He will make us clean from all the wrongs we have done.

1 JOHN 1:9

Thoughts to Grow On:

Have you ever done something you were ashamed of? You felt yucky inside from your throat to your gut. Worst of all, you couldn't "undo" it. It was done, and that's that.

You may have felt this about a sin you've done. You feared telling anyone about it—especially God. You imagined that he'd be so mad about it that he'd reject you forever.

Listen. God isn't like that at all. Yes, God hates the bad thing you did, but he loves *you*. He wants you to come to him and confess—that means, tell him—when you do something wrong. He wants you to admit that you did something wrong so that he can make everything right again.

Today:
Confess your sins to God.

🌐 MY AMAZING WORLD 🌐

Soap has been around for more than 1,000 years. It was first used by tribes from Germany.

Sing a New Song to God

△ ◓ ▢ △ ○ ▢ △ ○ ▢

BIBLE VERSE

Sing to the Lord a new song. Sing to the Lord, all the earth.

PSALM 96:1

Thoughts to Grow On:

Do you like to sing? Think about some of your favorite songs. How do they make you feel when you sing them?

Some people have noticed they feel happier and more energetic when they sing a song. Even in the cruel days of slavery, the slaves found strength, hope, and power by singing. The apostle Paul and Silas found joy and strength in the midst of their sufferings by singing, too.

God wants YOU to make up *new* songs and sing them to him. These songs will give you power and joy, and will be like a sweet aroma to God.

Today:

Sing a new song to God.

MY AMAZING WORLD

Humpback whales have been recorded "singing." Their songs last from six minutes to as long as 30 minutes! Their songs can be heard underwater for hundreds of miles.

Satan Is a Thief

△ ◉ ▢ ◣ ◯ ▣ ◣ ◉ ▢

BIBLE VERSE

"A thief comes to steal and kill and destroy."

JOHN 10:10

Thoughts to Grow On:

The Bible describes the devil as a *"roaring lion looking for someone to eat"* (1 Peter 5:8)—something you definitely want to try to avoid. Jesus gives you three clues to determine if something is from the devil.

1. If it will "*steal*" anything of yours, such as your honesty or your innocence, it is of the devil.

2. If it will "*kill*" anything of yours, such as your hope

or your desire to do good,
it is of the devil.

3. If it will *"destroy"*
   anything of yours, such as
   your good reputation or
   your faith, it is of the devil.

Satan wants to ruin your life.
Jesus wants to bless your life.
When you choose Jesus' way, you
win a great victory over the devil.

Today:
Seek a blessed life in Jesus!

MY AMAZING WORLD

Not only does a skunk's spray stink, it can
make you temporarily blind, too.

Share

BIBLE VERSE

Do not forget to do good to others. And share with them what you have.

HEBREWS 13:16

Thoughts to Grow On:

Sometimes sharing feels like giving something up that you were planning to have *all for yourself.* Everything in you wants to scream, "But it's *MINE!*" Sometimes sharing means risking that something you love might be lost, used up, or broken. Who'd be excited about doing that?

Aha! There is another side to sharing that actually makes you feel better. This happens when you decide to put someone else's happiness *ahead* of your own. As strange as it sounds, putting *others'* happiness first is the surest way to happiness for yourself. God made it so that we would *receive* by *giving*.

Today:

Share something with someone and see how you feel.

 MY AMAZING WORLD

The "Toys for Tots" program seeks to give every child the simple joy of a new toy for Christmas. It began in 1947, and has collected and given more than 100 million toys to children.

Jesus Is Coming Back

△ ● ■ △ ○ ■ △ ● ■

BIBLE VERSE

"Men of Galilee, why are you standing here looking
into the sky? You saw Jesus taken away from
you into heaven. He will come back in the
same way you saw him go."

ACTS 1:11

Thoughts to Grow On:

How would you feel if you
were told that a dear
friend you haven't seen in
a very long time was
coming to your house?
Can you imagine how
excited you would be?

More than 2,000 years ago,
Jesus was lifted up into heaven.
The apostles watched as he went
up into the sky and out of sight.

Here's the great part: He's coming back! Jesus Christ is coming back to this earth some day to share his love with you.

Today:

Look up at the sky today and imagine how exciting it will be to watch Jesus come down from the clouds.

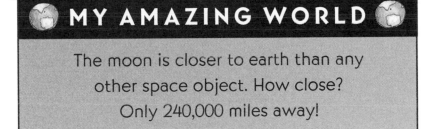

🌎 MY AMAZING WORLD 🌎

The moon is closer to earth than any other space object. How close? Only 240,000 miles away!

Subject Index

Abel (and Cain), 158–159
Adam (and Eve), 140
affection, 120
agapé, 120–121
allowance, 58
angel, 154, 155
anger(y) (ily), 9, 30, 32, 33, 54, 55,
    132, 145, 146, 153, 159, 177
ant, 136
apostle(s), 98, 200
    Paul (the apostle), 99, 195
    Peter (the apostle), 150, 170–171
argument(s), 54, 124
bad thoughts, 70–71
best friend(s), 18, 39, 65, 135, 142,
    189
bike, 94
birds, 29, 81, 157, 161
birthday, 51, 56–58, 173
bitter(ness), 36, 114, 158, 159, 177
blind, 67, 115
Cain (and Abel), 158
Cat in the Hat, The, 152
caterpillar, 4
Christ, 57
    See Jesus
Christmas, 51, 130, 199
clothes, 40, 72–73, 84, 118, 188
confess, 192, 193
conscience, 46
courage, 23, 46
Creator, 64
cross, 39, 177
danger(ous), 111, 169
dark(ness), 96–97, 162, 163
deaf, 67, 157
death, 18, 39, 154–155, 169
devil, 78, 118, 119, 191, 196

(as a) roaring lion, 196
(as) Satan, 196, 197
    See Tasmanian (Amazing Facts Index)
dirty joke, 48, 49
dirty word, 48, 49
discernment, 82–83
discouraged, 26, 86, 87, 182, 183
dominoes, 164–165
Dorcas. See Tabitha
Emperor's New Suit, The, 40
endorphins, 88
Eve. See Adam
faith(ful), 68, 74, 98, 107, 151, 169,
    197
farmer, 6–7
fashions, 40
flashlight, 96–97, 162
forgive(ness), 10, 27, 81, 107, 145,
    176, 192
friend(s), 18, 34, 46, 56, 65, 85, 87,
    93, 108, 113, 134–135, 142, 150,
    157, 162, 170, 177, 188–189,
    200
friendship(s), 35, 39, 93, 135, 176
frogs, 129, 154
genius, 172
gift(s), 42, 43, 56, 57, 61, 121, 74,
    172
grasshopper, 136
grumble, 12, 16
guilt(y), 20, 21
happy, 3, 14, 36, 37, 30, 39, 89,
    106, 107, 122, 123
happier, 194
happiest, 60
happily, 59
happiness, 21, 199, 100, 61
heart, 6, 10, 20, 21, 29, 38, 47, 59,

Scripture Index

Amazing Facts Index

More amazing facts to fascinate your friends!

If you could swim to the bottom of the ocean, you just might see a line of lobsters walking single file (as many as 60), with each lobster gently holding on to the one in front of it. Call it a "lobster train," if you'd like. Amazingly, these lobster trains can walk as far as 10 miles in a single day. Wow!

Picnic attendees beware: The average mosquito has 47 teeth. Ouch!

Which is stronger: The strongest man in the world or a honeybee?
Answer: The honeybee.
Why? The honeybee can lift 300 times its own weight. In order for a man to do that, he would have to be able to lift 15 tons!

An ostrich's eye is bigger than its brain.

Bullfrogs close their nostrils and breathe through their skin while under water.

Bald eagles use their nests for many years. Each year they make it stronger by adding twigs and branches. Many bald eagles' nests are as large as 20 feet deep and as wide as nine feet across, and one 34-year-old nest weighed in at more than two tons!

Octopuses and squid have three hearts!

The male giraffe not only has the longest neck of any other animal, but it also has the longest tail. Some giraffe tails have grown as long as eight feet!

More fun things for you to do!

In a separate journal, do the following:

★ Find and list your own fabulous factoids that will
   fascinate your friends!

★ Write down ten of your favorite Bible verses,
   and memorize them.

★ List your growing experiences! Here's an example:

Today *I disagreed with Jason about the rules of a game.*

I grew because *instead of arguing with him, we read the*
rules together. Sure enough, he was right.